ROOTED
in
FAITH

12 PROVEN WAYS TO DEEPEN YOUR
RELATIONSHIP WITH GOD AND
OVERCOME LIFE'S CHALLENGES

PAUL OKWECHIME

ROOTED IN FAITH: 12 Proven Ways to Deepen Your Relationship with God and Overcome Life's Challenges

Copyright © March 2025 by
Empowered 4 Wealth Publishing

Published by:
Empowered 4 Wealth Publishing

All rights reserved. No part of this book may be reproduced without the publisher's written permission, except for brief excerpts used for reviews, articles, or academic purposes.

For further information or permissions, contact:
Empowered 4 Wealth Publishing
Email: info@empoweredforwealth.com
Website: www.empoweredforwealth.com

Connect with Empowered 4 Wealth:

 @Empowered4WealthPublishing

 @Empowered4Wealth_publishing

Contents

Introduction v

Chapter 1   Building on the Rock 1
Chapter 2   Surrendering to God 7
Chapter 3   Hearing God's Voice 13
Chapter 4   Beauty from Ashes 21
Chapter 5   Trusting God in the Valley 29
Chapter 6   Overcoming Doubt and Fear 37
Chapter 7   Abiding in Christ 45
Chapter 8   Serving Others in Love 51
Chapter 9   Sharing Your Faith 59
Chapter 10 Growing in Community 67
Chapter 11 Living a Life of Worship 75
Chapter 12 Pressing On Toward the Goal 83

Conclusion: A Lifelong Journey of Growth 87
Next Steps & Call to Action 89
Acknowledgments 93
About the Author 95

Introduction

What if every challenge, every moment of doubt, and every hardship you've faced was part of a greater purpose?

The Christian journey is not just about surviving life's storms—it's about thriving through them, finding strength in God's promises, and experiencing transformation in the process. Whether you're searching for hope in uncertain times, longing for deeper faith, or simply trying to understand the struggles you face, this book is your companion. Together, we'll explore how to build firm faith, surrender with trust in God, and walk confidently through life's valleys with God by your side.

The Christian journey is a growth path filled with challenges, moments of transformation, joy, and victories. It is a path of development, often marked by trials that shape us and deepen our relationship with God. Our faith provides a strong foundation during uncertain times, comfort in grief, and overcoming strength during hardships.

Yet spiritual growth is not always easy. It requires surrender, trust, and a willingness to embrace God's plans, even when they seem unclear. This growth process often involves facing personal struggles, doubts, and fears. These moments serve as opportunities to draw us closer to God, rely on His promises, and experience His love more profoundly.

Just as a deeply rooted tree withstands the fiercest storms, a believer anchored in God's promises through faith will remain standing after the storms of life.

This book is designed to accompany you as you grow in your faith. It includes stories, insights, and biblical truths to encourage and inspire you. Each chapter explores a vital aspect of the Christian journey, offering practical steps to help you apply your faith in everyday life.

Every believer's story is unique. The struggles and victories you experience are part of a greater purpose—an eternal weight of glory that far exceeds your imagination (2 Corinthians 4:17). This book is intended to help you remain rooted in faith and remind you of God's presence and your victory in every season of life—Faith is your victory. It encourages you to explore a deeper relationship with Christ and to rediscover your sense of purpose through real-life testimonies, scriptural guidance, and moments of reflection. As you embark on this journey, consider asking yourself: How is God calling you to grow in faith today?

CHAPTER 1

Building on the Rock

As we embark on this journey of spiritual growth, laying a firm and unshakable foundation in God's Word is essential. This foundation on God's Word is the bedrock of our faith, providing security and confidence.

Jesus expressly discussed the immutability of God's Word in Matthew 24:35. He said that even if Heaven and Earth pass away, my words will not pass away, making His word a reliable basis upon which to build. He also highlighted the value of a firm foundation in Matthew 7:24-27. A wise builder places their house on the rock, not shifting sand. This analogy underscores the necessity of rooting our faith in the unshakable truth of God's Word.

Trusting in God's Character

Trusting God begins with understanding His character—God is good, faithful, just, and unchanging. His promises endure through generations. Building on this foundation means acting on His Word, aligning your life with His Word, trusting His plan, and believing in His goodness.

When we cultivate a relationship with God and act on His Word, our priorities shift from self-centered goals to Christ-centered ones. Seeking His kingdom above all else provides us with stability and fulfillment. Problems don't seem insurmountable anymore. God's presence strengthens us by bringing peace and directing our decisions.

Living Out God's Word

It takes deliberate effort to implement this truth. A wise man once said repetition is the law of deep and lasting impression, which implies that spiritual growth is promoted by the everyday practice of God's word.

Prayer strengthens our relationship with God, scripture reading broadens our understanding, and declaring His word brings it to pass in our lives. Worship refocuses our hearts on God's greatness. These habits build a strong basis for overcoming obstacles in life.

As believers, we are not alone in our journey. Our faith flourishes in the community of believers. Just as Hebrews 10:25 teaches us not to neglect meeting together because, in our meetings, we encourage one another, offering support and accountability

–iron sharpens iron. Sharing both burdens and victories serves as a reminder of God's faithfulness. Together, as the Church, we strengthen our individual faith through fellowship and teaching.

Reflecting on our life foundations offers valuable insights for growth. A weak foundation highlights areas that require attention, while a strong foundation demonstrates the power of God's Word in action. Both situations create opportunities for deeper trust and surrender to God's plans.

Each believer is a builder, constructing their spiritual house. The materials we choose—faith, obedience, trust—determine the strength of our structure. The only true and reliable rock is God's truth, and every step taken in faith builds something eternal.

Reflection & Application: Building on the Rock

As you consider the importance of a strong foundation in faith, take a moment to evaluate your position.

Are you building on the solid ground of God's Word, or is your faith being challenged by life's storms?

Reflection Questions

What are some areas in your life where your foundation feels unsteady?

Are there fears, doubts, or challenges that shake your faith? Identify them and bring them before God.

- _____
- _____
- _____
- _____
- _____
- _____
- _____

How can you actively build your faith in God's Word this week?

Consider incorporating Bible study, prayer, or worship into your daily routine to strengthen your spiritual foundation.

- _____
- _____
- _____
- _____
- _____

In what ways has trusting God changed your perspective in past challenges?

Recall moments when God has been faithful in your life. How did those experiences deepen your trust in Him?

- _____
- _____
- _____
- _____
- _____
- _____

CHAPTER 2

SURRENDERING TO GOD

Again and again—perhaps a hundred, even two hundred times—I repeated the phrase: *"I have a sound mind."* Until my breakthrough came, I kept God's truth on my lips. I reminded myself that everything else was temporary and unreal, but His Word was eternal. And in time, it became my reality.

Jesus (the Word) said in John 14:6, "I am the way, The Truth, and The Life." I learned this law: speak God's promises and completely trust His word in moments of doubt and fear. This may sound easier said than done, but that was how I got free from a health challenge in my teenage years –it is possible to silence the voice of fear with the truth by voicing God's Word.

Surrender is at the heart of a growing faith. It means letting go of control and trusting entirely in God. Surrender is not a one-time decision but a daily posture of the heart. It reflects humility, faith, and reliance on God's wisdom over personal understanding.

True surrender involves letting go of self-reliance. Human nature leans toward control, striving to shape circumstances and outcomes. This tendency often leads to frustration and exhaustion. Surrender offers freedom from the weight of trying to control what only God can handle.

Scripture calls believers to surrender with trust and confidence. Proverbs 3:5-6 emphasizes trusting in the Lord with all your heart and not leaning on your own understanding. This passage teaches that surrendering to God is an act of faith, acknowledging God's faithfulness, superior knowledge, and perfect timing.

Obedience flows naturally from surrender. When we fully submit our hearts to God, His commands are clear and desirable. Surrender allows one to live according to His will, even when it challenges our comfort or personal plans.

Surrender does not eliminate struggles; It changes our perspective on challenges. Trusting God allows believers to face uncertainty with peace. Psalm 46:10 invites believers to be still and know that He is God. Stillness creates space for God's presence to calm fears and provide clarity.

One practical example of surrender was when I asked God for a request in prayer.

SURRENDERING TO GOD
MY SURRENDER

There was a time I prayed fervently about a concern that weighed heavily on my heart. In response, God impressed upon me a simple truth: *Let Me handle it.*

Time passed, but the fears kept coming in the form of thoughts.

This scripture came to my heart, and just like Philippians 4:6 teaches us not to be anxious about anything *but to present our requests to God with thanksgiving.* With this in my heart, every time the worried thought came rushing in, I started to thank the Lord, saying; I'm not going to worry about that. The Lord has taken care of that concern, and I know what to do. That process for me was a fight of faith; as the worried thought kept coming back over again, I kept thanking the Lord even more until, after a while, calm and peace filled my heart, and there was no more worry, and it was clear what to do about that situation.

I learned surrendering to God's unfailing Word and holding fast to speaking his promises, with thanksgiving, will establish them in our lives.

Through this experience, I discovered that surrendering to God goes beyond a one-time decision; it becomes a daily practice that brings transformation. Practicing gratitude as an act of trust in God's provision and care.

Surrender produces spiritual fruit; a surrendered life bears the marks of peace, patience, and joy, and God works through those who yield to Him, using them to accomplish His purposes. Surrender aligns your heart with His will, allowing His power to transform your life.

ROOTED IN FAITH

God's faithfulness sustains the surrendered heart. He provides strength for every challenge and wisdom for every decision. His promises are trustworthy, and His plans are always good. Surrendering to Him brings rest, renewal, and purpose in every season of life.

Reflection & Application: Embracing a Life of Surrender

Key Takeaways:

My most important realizations from this chapter:

- _____
- _____
- _____
- _____

Next Steps:

Actions I will take to surrender more fully to God:

- _____
- _____
- _____
- _____

Areas for Growth:

Where do I need more faith, wisdom, or practical steps?

- _____

- _____

- _____

- _____

A Truth I Don't Want to Forget:

One key thought I want to hold onto:

- _____

- _____

- _____

CHAPTER 3

Hearing God's Voice

As a child, I remember sitting under a table, determined not to come out until God spoke to me for the first time. I waited a long time. Looking back now, I can't help but laugh. Years later, I can hardly go an hour without hearing His precious voice lovingly guiding me.

So, what is the secret to hearing His voice?

Be full of God's Spirit. In Ephesians 5:18, we are instructed not to get drunk on wine, as it can lead to reckless behavior, but to be filled by the Spirit.

Just as a drunk man is moved by wine to speak and act in ways he usually would not, being filled with God's Spirit makes it natural to think like him, speak his thoughts, and be led by God's Spirit.

This idea emphasizes the importance of staying filled with God's Spirit. God resides and is honored in the praise of His people. Psalm 22:3 highlights that God delights in your praise and thanksgiving. Additionally, Ephesians 5:19 reveals that singing and making a melody to the Lord from your heart is one way to engage with God and attune your ears to hear Him more clearly.

How God Speaks

Hearing God's voice is an important part of growing your faith. He speaks to us in many ways, offering guidance, encouragement, and truth when needed.

Recognizing His voice requires an open heart and a willingness to listen. When you take the time to hear Him, your faith strengthens, your trust in Him deepens, and you start seeing your life align more with His plan.

One of the main ways God speaks is through His Word. The Bible holds His timeless truths, offering wisdom and guidance for every aspect of your life. When we regularly read and meditate on scripture, it creates a foundation for discerning His voice. Just like sheep hear and obey their shepherd's voice, we, as God's sheep, have the innate ability to hear and obey his voice. Scripture describes His Word as a lamp to our feet and a light to our path (Psalm 119:105), providing clarity in moments of uncertainty. God's Word is Spirit, and the more we listen, the easier it is to hear his voice.

Prayer isn't just about talking to God and listing our requests—it's a two-way conversation. Taking time to listen creates space for Him to speak into our hearts. Sometimes, in the quiet moments, we hear Him the clearest.

Remember Elijah's story in 1 Kings 19:11-13? God didn't speak to him in the wind, the earthquake, or the fire but in a gentle whisper. God often speaks to us in this way, too—softly and subtly, when we slow down and make room for Him.

The Holy Spirit is also a huge part of how God communicates with us. Jesus promised that the Spirit would guide us into all truth (John 16:13). Whether through a gentle nudge, a feeling of conviction, or a deep sense of peace, the Holy Spirit is always at work, leading and encouraging us. The more we pay attention to these moments, the more we learn to recognize His voice and follow His lead.

Are you saved? You might say yes, but what gives you that assurance? God's Word teaches that His Spirit confirms with your spirit that you are His child. This inner conviction also helps you recognize His voice. However, praying and ensuring that everything aligns with Scripture is essential, as God's guidance will never contradict His Word.

Taking this thought a step further, I remember a time when I was unsure about a major decision. I prayed and sought clarity, but all I felt was silence. Doubts crept in, making me wonder if I was hearing from God. But as I spent time in prayer and scripture, I noticed a consistent message in His Word (Rhema) that aligned with a sense of peace in my heart. Looking back, I realized God had been speaking all along, guiding me through His Word and the gentle assurance of the Holy Spirit.

The Community of believers can offer additional clarity. Fellow believers provide wise counsel and confirmation of God's voice. Proverbs 15:22 reminds us that plans succeed with wise advisers. Talking things through with our Christian leaders provides accountability and helps discern God's direction.

Developing the ability to hear God takes time and practice. Familiarity with scripture enhances recognition of His voice. Setting aside distractions and creating dedicated time for prayer cultivates attentiveness. Journaling can capture impressions, scripture, and moments of clarity for further reflection.

Hearing God's voice isn't always easy. Doubt, fear, and the busyness of life can make it hard to listen. But when you recognize these obstacles and make an intentional effort to seek His presence, breakthroughs happen. Trusting that God wants to speak to you brings comfort, even when He feels distant.

Hearing God's voice transforms the journey of faith. His guidance brings peace in decisions, comfort in struggles, and purpose in every step. Learning to hear Him builds a relationship of trust and intimacy, anchoring life in His unchanging truth.

Reflection & Application: Hearing God's Voice

As you consider the importance of recognizing and responding to God's voice, take a moment to evaluate how you are listening.

Are you creating space in your life to hear Him, or is His voice being drowned out by distractions?

Reflection Questions

How has God spoken to you in the past?

Recall a time when you felt His leading, whether through Scripture, prayer, the Holy Spirit, or wise counsel. How did you recognize His voice?

- _____
- _____
- _____
- _____
- _____
- _____

What distractions or obstacles prevent you from hearing God's voice clearly?

Identify any fears or distractions that prevent you from hearing Him. What steps can you take to remove these barriers?

- _____

- _____

- _____

- _____

- _____

How can you actively grow in hearing God's voice this week?

Think of practical ways to tune in—whether through prayer, meditating on Scripture, worship, or journaling.

- _____

- _____

- _____

- _____

- _____

HEARING GOD'S VOICE

What is one thing God may be speaking to you about right now?

Take time to reflect and write down any impressions, scriptures, or guidance He may be revealing to you.

- _____

- _____

- _____

- _____

- _____

CHAPTER 4

Beauty from Ashes

God has a remarkable way of turning pain into purpose. Life may bring moments of heartbreak, loss, and despair, but these seasons are not without hope. God's ability to create beauty from ashes is a testament to His redemptive power. Isaiah 61:3 assures us that He will give "a crown of beauty instead of ashes, the oil of joy instead of mourning, and a garment of praise instead of a spirit of despair."

Pain is an inevitable part of the human experience. It often leaves wounds that feel too deep to heal. Yet, God meets His children in their brokenness. He does not waste a single moment of suffering but works through it to bring about transformation. His plans are higher than humans can understand, weaving even the darkest times into a greater purpose.

In moments of grief, our suffering reveals the depth of God's compassion, and His presence becomes tangible. Psalm 34:18 declares that the Lord is near to the brokenhearted and saves those whose spirits are crushed. His presence brings comfort and peace, even in challenging circumstances. As Psalm 16:11 says, there is fullness of joy in His presence. Therefore, it is wise during times of grief to seek and abide in God's presence, filling your joy tank.

Faith grows through trials.

Though God is not the author of confusion, we face an adversary—Satan—who seeks to sow destruction. Nevertheless, adversity compels us to rely on God's strength and wisdom. James 1:2-4 encourages believers to consider trials as pure joy because they produce perseverance and maturity. Difficult seasons refine our faith, revealing God's faithfulness and helping us build trust in His character. It is well known that fire does not destroy gold; it only purifies and glorifies it. Similarly, 2 Corinthians 4:17 reveals to us that if trials are handled with faith, they will only result in your greatness and glory.

Testimonies of redemption inspire hope.

Stories about how God has transformed pain into purpose in our lives remind others of His goodness. These testimonies serve as a source of light in the darkness. By sharing our personal experiences of healing, restoration, and growth, we can encourage those who are still navigating their struggles.

The psalmist captures this idea in Psalm 119:24, where he reflects on how filling his thoughts with testimonies of triumph enhances his understanding. As a result, he never lost a battle in his entire life.

Finding beauty in ashes requires surrender. Letting go of anger, bitterness, and fear opens the heart to God's healing work. Trusting Him to bring purpose from pain creates space for growth and renewal. As 2 Corinthians 12:9 states, His power is made perfect in our weakness, shining brightly through the cracks of our brokenness.

Scripture anchors on hope in difficult times. Promises of restoration and renewal provide assurance that God is at work, even when circumstances feel overwhelming. Meditating on verses like Romans 8:28, which declares that God orchestrates everything to work together for your good, will strengthen your faith in His redemptive plan. I pray in line with Joel 2:25-26 for God's restoration in your life.

Healing as a Process and a Gift

Healing is both a process and a gift. God's timing often differs from human expectations, but His work is always perfect. Healing does not erase the past but transforms it, allowing the scars of pain to tell a story of grace and redemption. Trusting in His ability to create beauty will enable believers to move forward with hope.

God can turn our pain into something beautiful. He brings light where there is darkness, showing us His love and power. This change can inspire others and draw them to Him. When we trust God during difficult times, we can experience true transformation and find a new sense of purpose. God promises to turn our ashes into beauty and always keeps that promise.

Reflection & Application: Beauty from Ashes

As you reflect on the ways God brings beauty from pain, take a moment to examine how He has worked in your life.

Reflection Questions

Where in your life have you seen God bring beauty from ashes?

Think of a time when you experienced hardship or loss but later saw God use it for good. How did that experience strengthen your faith?

- _____
- _____
- _____
- _____
- _____
- _____

ROOTED IN FAITH

Are there areas of brokenness in your life that you still need to surrender to God?

Identify any pain, grief, or burdens you are still carrying. What steps can you take to trust God with these struggles and allow Him to bring healing?

- _____

- _____

- _____

- _____

- _____

How can your story of healing encourage others?

Testimonies of God's restoration bring hope. How can you use your journey to uplift and inspire someone else who may be struggling?

- _____

- _____

- _____

- _____

- _____

What scriptures or promises of God bring you comfort during difficult times?

List verses that have helped you find peace and strength in seasons of hardship. Consider memorizing them or keeping them close for encouragement.

- _____

- _____

- _____

- _____

- _____

- _____

CHAPTER 5

TRUSTING GOD IN THE VALLEY

*L*ife often brings seasons of darkness and uncertainty—moments when the path forward feels obscured. These valleys test our faith, patience, and perseverance. Trusting God during these times becomes an act of surrender and reliance on His presence and promises. Even in the deepest valleys, God walks with His children, offering comfort, guidance, and hope (Psalm 23:4).

Valleys are inevitable. Scripture never promises a life free from hardship, but it assures us that God will never leave or forsake us. With Him, we can overcome.

Deuteronomy 31:6 has been a pillar of strength in my own life; knowing He is with me has made all the difference. Just as a child feels confident when their parents are present, even in the face of bullies or danger, having faith that God will always be by your side brings comfort, courage, and assurance. Challenges manifest in various ways—loss, disappointment, fear, and uncertainty—but none are beyond God's reach. His faithfulness remains constant, even when our circumstances feel overwhelming.

Trusting God in the valley requires remembering His character. God is unchanging, faithful, and compassionate. The same God who parted the sea, provided manna in the wilderness, and raised Christ from the dead is present in every trial. His power and love are sufficient for every challenge. As Ephesians 3:20 says, His power at work in you is greater than any challenge or obstacle you may face. And Greater is He in you than he that is in the world.

Scripture offers assurance in seasons of struggle. Psalm 23 paints a vivid picture of God's care, even in the valley of the shadow of death. The psalmist declares that God's rod and staff bring comfort, guidance, and protection through every difficulty. Meditating on His promises strengthens our faith. King David, in Psalm 43:5, spoke himself out of despair and into joy and praise. We can do the same.

God's presence is often most evident in the valleys of our lives. Pain and uncertainty create an opportunity for us to rely on Him. It's like a reminder to place our trust in Him.

King David, a man who overcame many challenges, said in Psalm 56:3, "When I am afraid, I will put my trust in you." The act of trusting Him brings peace, and His peace surpasses all understanding (Philippians 4:7), guarding our hearts and minds even when external circumstances remain chaotic. Trusting in His presence provides us with strength and courage.

TRUSTING GOD IN THE VALLEY

FAITH GROWS DEEPER IN THE VALLEY.

I remember my decision as if it were yesterday. I chose to trust God's word alone for my healing. In that frail state, and with symptoms evident in my body, I embarked on a journey of faith to learn how to receive divine healing for my body. At first, all I had was hope. I stumbled many times, but as Proverbs 24:16 says, a righteous person will get back up again. Then, I discovered powerful truths in God's Word. In 2 Timothy 1:7, I learned that I had a sound mind, and in Isaiah 53:4, I found that Jesus took my pain upon Himself when He died for me on the cross. I committed to meditating on and speaking His Word continually. Though perhaps a year passed, eventually, when I finally saw and believed my healing came—the truth made me free; God's word never fails.

When we face challenges with faith, these trials can refine and strengthen our reliance on God. They help reduce our dependence on ourselves and teach us humility. James 1:2-4 encourages believers to view difficulties as opportunities for growth, promoting perseverance and maturity. Challenging times shape our character and deepen our spiritual connection with God.

Trusting God during difficult times requires intentional practice. Prayer is a vital way to connect with His peace and wisdom. In these moments, worship helps shift our focus from our problems to God's greatness. As King David expressed in Psalm 119:99, reflecting on His past faithfulness brings enlightenment and builds our confidence in His ability to provide for both our present and future needs. Additionally, journaling can help us capture the lessons we've learned and remind us of His work in our lives.

The community of believers also provides support in the valley. Fellow believers can be a beacon of hope, offering encouragement, prayer, and accountability. Sharing burdens with others allows God's love to flow through His people.

Ecclesiastes 4:9-10 highlights the strength found in companionship, reminding us that two are better than one because they can help each other up. Many times, just coming to church and staying in God's presence can bring relief and healing.

The valley does not last forever. Psalm 30:5 says, "Weeping may last for the night, but joy comes in the morning." Soon, the challenges you're facing will turn into a testimony—stay in faith. God's promises of restoration bring us hope even in the darkest seasons. He works all things together for our good (Romans 8:28), redeeming our pain for His purposes. The journey through the valley leads to renewal, strength, and a closer walk with Him.

Trusting God in the valley reveals His faithfulness and strengthens our relationship with Him. His guidance, comfort, and promises remain unwavering regardless of our challenges. While valleys can be tough, they are part of the journey toward spiritual growth and serve as a testament to His ability to bring life, hope, and purpose in every season.

Reflection & Application: Trusting God in the Valley

As you reflect on the valleys in your life, consider how God has been present in those difficult moments.

Reflection Questions

What valleys have you walked through in your life?

Think about a difficult season you have faced. How did it test your faith, and how did God show His presence?

- _____
- _____
- _____
- _____
- _____
- _____

What is one way you can strengthen your trust in God during hard times?

Consider practices such as prayer, scripture meditation, worship, or seeking encouragement from fellow believers.

- _____
- _____
- _____
- _____
- _____

How has God shown His faithfulness to you in past struggles?

Reflect on moments where God has provided, comforted, or guided you. How does remembering these experiences help you trust Him more today?

- _____
- _____
- _____
- _____
- _____

Who can you encourage during their valley season?

Is there someone in your life going through a difficult time? How can you offer support, prayer, or words of encouragement?

- _____

- _____

- _____

- _____

- _____

- _____

CHAPTER 6

Overcoming Doubt and Fear

Doubt and fear are common struggles in the journey of faith. They can creep in during seasons of uncertainty, challenge convictions, and undermine trust in God. Overcoming these obstacles is a vital part of spiritual growth, requiring intentional reliance on God's truth and the courage to trust Him in all circumstances.

Understanding Doubt

Doubt often begins as a question. It can arise as a question about God's goodness, plans, Word, or presence during difficult times. In Genesis 3:1, Satan deceived Eve by questioning God's Word, which led her to doubt. His strategy has not changed. We can shield ourselves by continually entrenching God's truth in our hearts through meditation.

Although these questions can be unsettling, they are not inherently harmful. When approached with humility, doubt can become an opportunity for growth, prompting believers to seek a deeper understanding and reliance on God.

On the other hand, fear is rooted in uncertainty and the unknown. It immobilizes, clouds judgment, and tempts believers to turn away from trust in God. Scripture acknowledges the reality of fear but repeatedly calls believers to take courage. Isaiah 41:10 reassures us with God's words, "Do not fear, for I am with you; do not be dismayed, for I am your God."

Statistically, "Fear Not" is found 365 times in the Bible. That is one "fear Not" for every day of the year.

Focusing on God's promises can help you overcome doubt and fear. His Word provides a firm foundation for trust and offers countless assurances of His faithfulness. Meditating on scriptures such as 2 Timothy 1:7, which declares that God has not given you a spirit of fear but of power, love, and a sound mind, strengthens faith and dispels fear.

Apostle Peter is the only person recorded in scripture to have walked on water like Jesus. He accomplished this by trusting in Jesus' word. However, as he began to look away and focus on the sea and the waves, doubt crept into his heart and started to sink (Matthew 14:30-31). If doubt comes from shifting our focus away from God's word, then faith—the opposite of doubt—can be cultivated by hearing and concentrating solely on God's word as the ultimate source of truth.

OVERCOMING DOUBT AND FEAR

Prayer serves as a powerful tool for overcoming doubt and fear. When Peter cried out, "Lord, save me," his prayer was vital; he might have perished without it. Honest prayers that remind God of His promises invite Him into our struggles, acknowledging our human weakness while seeking His strength. Psalm 138:2 says that God has exalted His Word even above His name, and therefore, He is obliged to respond when we voice His Word and call on His name. As many as call upon Jesus' name shall be saved. Jesus welcomed the prayer of the Father in Mark 9:24, who said, "I believe; help my unbelief!" God honors these prayers by providing peace and reassurance.

Worship and thanksgiving shift our focus from fear to faith. Worship diminishes the power of doubt and fear by magnifying God's greatness. It reminds believers of His sovereignty and goodness, fostering a spirit of trust and confidence. Worship transforms our perspective, lifting our eyes from earthly challenges to the eternal hope found in Christ.

The Christian plays a significant role in overcoming doubt and fear. Fellow believers provide encouragement, share wisdom, and offer prayers. Hebrews 10:24-25 calls us to spur one another on toward love and good deeds, emphasizing the importance of gathering together and strengthening one another.

Faith grows through action. Stepping out despite fear reinforces our trust in God. Peter walking on water (Matthew 14:28-31) illustrates this principle. Though fear caused him to sink, Jesus' response was immediate, lifting him back up. God honors steps of faith, no matter how small, and uses them to deepen reliance on Him.

Reflecting on God's past faithfulness builds confidence for the future. Remembering how He has provided, guided, and sustained us creates a foundation of trust. Gratitude for His past work combats fear of the unknown, anchoring faith in His unchanging character.

Overcoming doubt and fear is not about achieving perfect faith but consistently trusting God. His love casts out fear (1 John 4:18), His truth silences doubt, and His presence brings peace.

By leaning into His promises, believers can face challenges with courage, knowing that He is with us every step of the way.

Reflection & Application: Overcoming Doubt and Fear

Doubt and fear are common struggles in the journey of faith, but God has given us the tools to overcome them. Take a moment to reflect on how these challenges have affected your walk with Him.

Reflection Questions

What doubts or fears have been weighing on your heart?

Identify areas where uncertainty has challenged your faith. Find scriptures on this topic and declare God's word to that mountain - it will move.

- _____
- _____
- _____
- _____
- _____
- _____

How can you shift your focus from fear to faith?

Think of practical ways to replace fearful thoughts with God's promises, such as scripture meditation, prayer, or worship.

- _____
- _____
- _____
- _____
- _____

When has God helped you overcome fear in the past?

Reflect on moments where God's presence or His Word brought you peace. How does this encourage you today?

- _____
- _____
- _____
- _____
- _____

Who in your life needs encouragement to trust God in their struggles?

Consider how you can uplift others who may be struggling with doubt and fear. Jesus told Peter, "After you have overcome, strengthen others."

- _____
- _____
- _____
- _____
- _____
- _____

CHAPTER 7

Abiding in Christ

Abiding in Christ is essential for spiritual growth and fruitfulness. It is the practice of remaining deeply connected to Him, drawing strength, wisdom, and purpose from His presence. In John 15:1-8, Jesus describes this relationship, teaching that He is the vine and believers are the branches. Just as a branch cannot bear fruit apart from the vine, a believer cannot thrive without abiding in Christ.

Abiding begins with a relationship. Accepting Jesus as Savior establishes this connection, but nurturing the relationship is what sustains it. Abiding is not a passive state but an active commitment to remain close to Him through prayer, scripture, and obedience. This daily communion fosters intimacy and deepens our faith. This relationship has many benefits; just as a tree's life flows into its branches, the same life, health, righteousness, and peace found in Christ flow into the believer. We share one Spirit, life, and inheritance, and even His name (Mark 16:17).

Prayer anchors the abiding relationship. It is an ongoing conversation with God, keeping the lines of communication open. Consistent prayer invites His guidance, comfort, and wisdom into every moment. Jesus exemplified a life of prayer, frequently withdrawing to quiet places to connect with the Father (Luke 5:16). When we follow His example, we cultivate a spirit of dependence on God.

Scripture is essential for abiding in Christ, revealing God's character, will, and promises. Studying the Bible aligns our hearts with His truth and provides a solid foundation for our faith. Meditating on verses like Psalm 1:2-3, which likens a person who delights in the law of the Lord to a tree planted by streams of water, highlights the importance of being rooted in His Word.

Obedience stems from abiding in Christ. Jesus taught that those who love Him will keep His commands (John 14:15), demonstrating our trust in His wisdom and submission to His authority. This obedience allows His will to unfold in our lives and strengthens our connection to Him, reflecting a heart fully yielded to His leading.

James 2:23 illustrates this through Abraham, who believed in God and acted on that belief, becoming known as God's friend. His obedience was a true manifestation of faith, showing that genuine faith involves believing God's Word and acting on it fearlessly.

Abiding in Him naturally produces spiritual fruit. The fruit of the Spirit—love, joy, peace, patience, kindness, goodness, faithfulness, gentleness, and self-control—flows from a life connected to Christ (Galatians 5:22-23). These virtues reflect His character and draw others to Him, fulfilling God's purpose in and through every believer.

However, abiding in Christ requires intentionality. Distractions and a busy schedule can divert our focus. To maintain our connection, we must dedicate time to prayer, studying scripture, and worship. Practices like journaling, fasting, or joining a small group can also strengthen our commitment to Him.

The benefits of abiding are profound. It brings peace in times of uncertainty, strength in moments of weakness, and joy in every circumstance. Abiding transforms our hearts, aligning our desires with God's will. It provides clarity and direction, guiding our steps according to His purpose. Most importantly, abiding fosters a deep and unshakable relationship with Christ.

Abiding in Christ is a lifelong journey. It is not just about perfection but rather about persistence—continually seeking to remain in His presence. As we believers abide in Him, we grow in faith, produce fruit, and experience the fullness of life that only He can provide. Remaining in Him ensures that His love, grace, and power flow through every aspect of our lives, enabling us to live for His glory.

Reflection & Application – Abiding in Christ

Just as a branch must remain attached to its tree to thrive and receive nourishment, abiding in Christ is essential for a flourishing faith. Take a moment to consider how you can strengthen your relationship with Him.

Reflection Questions

What does abiding in Christ mean to you?

Think about how staying connected to Jesus has impacted your spiritual journey.

- _____
- _____
- _____
- _____
- _____
- _____
- _____

ABIDING IN CHRIST

What distractions keep you from staying connected to Christ?

Identify habits, worries, or commitments that may be pulling you away from your time with Him.

- _____

- _____

- _____

- _____

- _____

How can you be more intentional about abiding in Christ?

List practical steps such as setting aside quiet time, studying scripture, engaging in worship, or deepening your prayer life.

- _____

- _____

- _____

- _____

- _____

ROOTED IN FAITH

What fruit of the Spirit do you see growing in your life?

Reflect on how abiding in Christ has shaped your character and relationships.

- _____

- _____

- _____

- _____

- _____

CHAPTER 8

SERVING OTHERS IN LOVE

The call to serve others is at the heart of the Christian life. Jesus Himself modeled a life of service, humbling Himself to wash His disciples' feet and ultimately laying down His life for all. Helping others is not just a duty but a privilege and a profound way to demonstrate God's love to the world. In serving, we mirror Christ and fulfill the command to love our neighbors as ourselves (Matthew 22:39).

Serving others begins with a heart of compassion. Jesus looked at the crowds and had compassion for them, seeing them as sheep without a shepherd (Matthew 9:36). When we see others through Jesus' eyes, we begin to care about their physical, emotional, and spiritual needs. True compassion moves beyond sympathy—it inspires action. Genuine service is not about obligation; it flows from a heart that longs to meet the needs of others out of love.

Jesus taught that true greatness in His kingdom comes through serving others. In Mark 9:35, He said, "Anyone who wants to be first must be the very last, and the servant of all." This upside-down view of greatness challenges worldly perspectives, which prioritize power and recognition. In the Kingdom of God, greatness is found in humble service. Serving others may not bring fame or accolades, but it aligns the believer with God's will and heart.

Serving others requires sacrifice. It often means stepping out of our comfort zones and putting the needs of others before our own. Jesus demonstrated this by His willingness to give everything for humanity. His ultimate sacrifice on the cross is the greatest example of selfless service. In the same way, serving others requires time, energy, and sometimes resources. But God promises to honor sacrificial service and use it for His glory.

SMALL ACTS, ETERNAL IMPACT

Service is not limited to grand gestures. It can be as simple as offering a kind word, providing a meal, or helping someone in need. Even the smallest acts of kindness can have a profound impact. In Matthew 25:40, Jesus tells us that whatever we do for the least of His brothers and sisters, we do for Him. Every act of service, no matter how small, is significant in God's eyes. It is an opportunity to show His love in tangible ways.

Serving others also involves spiritual care. While meeting physical needs is essential, believers are also called to minister to the souls of others. Sharing the gospel, offering prayer, and encouraging others in their walk with God are vital aspects of service. It's about sharing the hope of Christ and leading others to Him, helping them grow in their faith.

Service isn't always easy. Sometimes, it involves loving and helping those who are difficult or who have hurt us. Yet, Jesus calls us to love even our enemies and pray for those who persecute us (Matthew 5:44). This radical love is a testimony to the world of God's transformative power. Choosing to serve difficult people reflects God's mercy and grace, demonstrating that His love is for everyone, regardless of their actions toward us.

Serving others is also a way to grow in humility. When we serve, we are reminded that we are not superior to those we help. We all stand on equal ground before God. Service strips away pride and reminds believers of the grace they have received from God. It fosters a spirit of humility and gratitude, recognizing that everything we have is a gift from God. Service also brings out the best in us.

Serving in God's house enables our dormant innate gifts.

When we step forward with a desire to serve, God often reveals abilities we never knew we had. I personally experienced this when I learned to play the piano while serving. My experiences building software, making music in the choir, and evangelizing for Jesus helped me acquire valuable skills that have proven to be highly rewarding.

Additionally, serving God has a positive impact on our overall health. One scripture that inspired me during a difficult time was Exodus 23:25. I prayed, saying, "Lord, heal me, and I will serve you." Almost instantly, I felt a surge of strength through my body. The symptoms disappeared, and I returned to my normal life—so much so that I even played basketball that same day.

Finally, serving others builds community. As described in Acts 2:44-45, the early Church was a community of believers who shared everything and met each other's needs. Serving others strengthens the body of Christ, fostering unity, love, and mutual support. When we serve together, we reflect the heart of God and build a community that reflects His love to the world.

Serving others is a natural expression of a life that is rooted in Christ and in love. It is both an act of obedience and an opportunity to grow in love, humility, and compassion. In the exact words of Jesus in John 13:34, *"Love each other. Just as I have loved you, so you must love one another."* When we serve, we become more like Him, reflecting His character and sharing His love with a broken world.

Whether in small, everyday acts or large, sacrificial service, every act of service is a way to honor God and further His Kingdom on earth.

Reflection & Application: Serving Others in Love

Service is a reflection of Christ's love. Consider how you can embrace a heart of service.

Reflection Questions

How has God called you to serve others?

Think of the ways you currently serve or could begin serving in your home, church, or community.

- _____
- _____
- _____
- _____
- _____
- _____
- _____
- _____

What holds you back from serving with love and humility?

Identify any fears, hesitations, or distractions that may be preventing you from stepping out in service.

- _____
- _____
- _____
- _____
- _____

What small acts of service can you incorporate into your daily life?

List ways you can show love through simple gestures of kindness and generosity.

- _____
- _____
- _____
- _____
- _____

SERVING OTHERS IN LOVE

Who in your life needs encouragement or help this week?

Think of someone who could benefit from your time, prayers, or support.

- _____
- _____
- _____
- _____
- _____

CHAPTER 9

Sharing Your Faith

Sharing our faith is one of a Christian's greatest privileges and responsibilities. The gospel—the good news of God's love, grace, and salvation through Jesus Christ—is a message meant to be shared. As believers, we are called to proclaim this truth, fulfilling the Great Commission Jesus gave in Matthew 28:19-20: "Go and make disciples of all nations."

Evangelism begins with a deep understanding of the gospel. It is the story of how God, in His love, sent Jesus to live a sinless life, die on the cross for humanity's sins, and rise again, offering eternal life to all who believe. Knowing and believing this truth is essential for effectively sharing it. The deeper a believer understands the gospel, the more confidently they can proclaim it.

Reaching out to friends and loved ones with this good news is one of the highest expressions of love. It shows that we truly care for them and desire for them to participate in the Kingdom of God and experience His grace and goodness.

Authenticity is key when sharing our faith. People are drawn to our genuine experiences and personal stories. Sharing what God has done in your own life makes the message relatable and real. Testimonies of transformation, healing, or guidance show how faith has made a tangible difference. This personal connection can open hearts to the truth of the gospel.

Evangelism is not limited to formal preaching. Everyday conversations provide opportunities to share our faith naturally. A kind word, a listening ear, or a moment of prayer can plant seeds of hope. Colossians 4:6 encourages believers to let our conversations always be full of grace and seasoned with salt so we may know how to answer everyone. Being intentional in everyday interactions allows God to use even small moments for His glory.

Fear of rejection or feelings of inadequacy often prevents believers from sharing their faith. It is essential to trust the Holy Spirit to lead and guide us. The Holy Spirit is the power of God, empowering us believers to speak boldly and providing the right words to say (Acts 1:8). Overcoming fear requires us to focus on God's power rather than our personal abilities. Sharing our faith is not about being perfect but about obeying and relying on His strength.

SHARING YOUR FAITH

Building relationships is an effective way to share our faith

People are more receptive to the gospel when they feel valued and understood. Investing in others' lives demonstrates Christ's love in action. Strong relationships foster trust, creating an environment where spiritual conversations can naturally develop over time. When we genuinely care for others, we often find opportunities to share the hope found in Christ. This is why He instructs us to love one another.

Scripture is a powerful tool in evangelism. God's Word communicates to the heart in ways that human words cannot. Sharing verses such as John 3:16 or Romans 10:9-10 lays a solid foundation for understanding salvation. Encouraging others to explore the Bible on their own invites them into a personal encounter with God.

Prayer is vital in sharing faith. Praying for those who do not yet know Christ softens their hearts and prepares them to receive the message. Prayer also empowers the one sharing and provides courage, guidance, and compassion. Ephesians 6:19-20 highlights the importance of prayer for boldness in proclaiming the gospel.

Living out our faith strengthens our message. Actions often speak louder than words. When others see kindness, patience, and love reflected in a believer's life, they experience the transformative power of the gospel. Matthew 5:16 encourages believers to let their light shine before others so that people may see our good deeds and glorify God. Just as a baby will eventually imitate their parents in words and actions, evangelism and bringing new converts into God's kingdom is like giving birth spiritually; our words and actions carry significant weight.

Rejection is a possible outcome, but it should not discourage believers. Jesus faced rejection, and He reminded His followers that they might experience the same (John 15:18-20).

Sharing our faith is not about controlling the outcome but about planting seeds and trusting God to bring growth. Even when responses are not immediate, God's Word never returns void (Isaiah 55:11).

Sharing faith is ultimately an act of love. It is an invitation for others to experience the hope, joy, and salvation found in Christ. Whether through conversations, actions, or prayers, every effort to share the gospel contributes to God's Kingdom. By stepping out in faith and obedience, believers participate in the transformative work of bringing others into a relationship with Jesus.

Reflection & Application: Sharing Your Faith

Sharing your faith is a powerful way to extend God's love to others. Take a moment to reflect on how you can boldly and effectively share the gospel.

Reflection Questions

Who in your life needs to hear the gospel?

Identify people in your circle—family, friends, or colleagues—who may be open to hearing about Jesus.

- _____
- _____
- _____
- _____
- _____
- _____
- _____

What holds you back from sharing your faith?

Are there fears, doubts, or obstacles that prevent you from speaking about Christ? How can you overcome them?

- _____
- _____
- _____
- _____
- _____

What's your personal testimony of faith?

Think about how God has transformed your life. How can you use your story to encourage and inspire others?

- _____
- _____
- _____
- _____
- _____

SHARING YOUR FAITH

How can you share your faith naturally in everyday conversations?

List ways to bring up faith in organic, relatable ways—through kindness, storytelling, and genuine interest in others.

- _____
- _____
- _____
- _____
- _____

What scripture can you share with someone who is searching for truth?

Find a Bible verse that speaks to salvation and encouragement.

- _____
- _____
- _____
- _____
- _____

CHAPTER 10

Growing in Community

Spiritual growth is not a solo journey. God intended for believers to develop and flourish within a community where they can support each other, share their challenges, and encourage one another in their faith. This was demonstrated in the early Church, as seen in Acts 2:42-47, where believers devoted themselves to fellowship, prayer, and breaking bread together, experiencing the power of unity and collective worship. Growing together in the community strengthens our faith and showcases God's love to the world.

There is a blessing In the gathering of believers.

Psalm 133:1-3 reminds us:

> *"How good and pleasant it is when God's people live together in unity! ... For there the LORD bestows His blessing—life forevermore."*

God delights in His people dwelling together in harmony, so much so that He commands a blessing over them. In this atmosphere of unity, we experience a corporate anointing, a divine empowerment that refreshes and uplifts our spirits.

I recall times when I didn't feel joyful or when I was sick, but after attending a church service, I would leave feeling refreshed. Additionally, being part of a community makes prayer and receiving answers easier as we unite our faith to agree on various matters. There is an ease, an anointing, and a blessing that comes from gathering with fellow believers.

Hebrews 10:25 reminds us: "Let us not neglect our meetings, as some people do." God values our church gatherings and encourages us to participate because His blessings await us there.

Being a part of a church provides essential support during challenging times. Life's difficulties can often feel overwhelming, but facing them alongside other believers offers comfort and hope. In Galatians 6:2, believers are encouraged to help carry each other's burdens, which fulfills Christ's commandment. A caring community reassures each member that they are not alone and that they have the support and prayers of God's family surrounding them.

Accountability is a vital aspect of the community. Fellow believers provide honest feedback, gentle correction, and encouragement to stay on the path of righteousness. Proverbs 27:17 states, "As iron sharpens iron, so one person sharpens another." Accountability fosters spiritual growth by helping individuals stay aligned with God's will and resist temptation.

Diversity in the community enriches faith. Each person brings unique gifts, perspectives, and experiences that contribute to the body of Christ. 1 Corinthians 12:12-27 describes believers as parts of one body, each with a distinct role and purpose. We realize that we need each other, and embracing our diversity in backgrounds, talents, and viewpoints deepens our understanding and appreciation of God's creativity and design.

Worshiping together strengthens the bond within the community. Corporate worship strengthens the bonds within a faith community. When believers gather to sing, pray, and study God's Word together, it magnifies the experience of His presence. Worship unites hearts and aligns them with His Spirit. Hebrews 10:24-25 emphasizes the importance of meeting together and encouraging one another, especially as the Day of the Lord approaches.

Serving one another in love and working together strengthens relationships and advances God's Kingdom. Our acts of service—whether feeding the hungry, caring for the sick, or supporting those in need—reflect Christ's love within us. Working together fosters deeper connections among believers and showcases God's compassion to the world. Through service, communities can transform into beacons of hope and light.

The church plays a vital role in helping individual believers discover and utilize our spiritual gifts. According to Matthew 25:15, God equips each believer with unique abilities to serve and glorify Him. A supportive community recognizes these gifts in individuals and offers opportunities for their expression. Additionally, encouragement from fellow believers fosters confidence, enabling each member to fulfill their God-given purpose.

Healthy conflict resolution strengthens the bonds among believers. Disagreements are inevitable in any group, but addressing them with humility and love encourages growth. Matthew 18:15-17 offers guidance for resolving conflicts in a manner that honors God and restores relationships. Addressing disputes with grace reflects Christ's teachings and enhances our unity.

Investing in the church community requires intentional effort.

Building strong relationships often takes time, commitment, and vulnerability. Joining a small group, participating in church activities, or mentoring others can create valuable opportunities for connection and self-development. Regularly showing up and engaging with others demonstrates your commitment to the body of Christ.

Ecclesiastes 4:12 illustrates this truth: *"Though one may be overpowered, two can defend themselves. A cord of three strands is not quickly broken."* Strength is found in unity, and isolation is one of the enemy's strategies to weaken believers. By staying connected, we resist division and stand firm in faith.

The church also reflects God's nature. As a relational God, He exists in perfect unity within the Trinity—Father, Son, and Holy Spirit. Believers reflect this divine relationship by living in harmony with one another. Loving one another, as Christ loved us, becomes a testimony to the world of God's transformative power.

Growing as part of the church community transforms our faith and positively impacts the world around us. It provides us with encouragement, accountability, and opportunities for worship and service. This fellowship shapes believers into Christ's likeness and magnifies His love through collective action.

By committing to the church, we believers fulfill God's design for us, glorifying Him together and advancing His Kingdom.

Reflection & Application – Growing in Community

Growing in faith is not meant to be a solitary journey. God created us for fellowship and community, where we can encourage, support, and strengthen one another. Take a moment to reflect on your engagement with your faith community.

Reflection Questions

How has being part of a faith community impacted your spiritual growth?

Reflect on how your church, small group, or Christian friendships have helped you grow in faith.

- _____

- _____

- _____

- _____

- _____

- _____

- _____

GROWING IN COMMUNITY

Are you actively engaging with your church or faith community?

What steps can you take to be more involved through fellowship, serving, or mentoring?

- _____
- _____
- _____
- _____
- _____

How can you be a source of encouragement to someone in your faith community this week?

Think of someone needing support, prayer, or a word of encouragement. How can you show them God's love?

- _____
- _____
- _____
- _____
- _____

What spiritual gifts has God given you that could be used to bless the community?

Consider how you can use your unique talents to serve others.

- _____
- _____
- _____
- _____
- _____

What obstacles, if any, have kept you from fully committing to a faith community?

Identify any barriers and pray for wisdom on how to overcome them.

- _____
- _____
- _____
- _____
- _____

CHAPTER 11

LIVING A LIFE OF WORSHIP

Worship is more than singing songs or attending church services—it is a way of life. True worship flows from a heart that recognizes God's greatness, goodness, and sovereignty. It encompasses every aspect of our daily lives, reflecting our devotion to Him. Romans 12:1 urges believers to offer their bodies as living sacrifices, holy and pleasing to God—this, Scripture says, is our true and proper worship. When we live with this mindset, every moment becomes an opportunity to glorify Him.

ROOTED IN FAITH

Our daily actions reflect a life of worship.

Worship is not confined to Sunday services or specific rituals. It includes how believers live, work, serve, and interact with others. Colossians 3:17 urges us believers to do everything in the name of the Lord Jesus, giving thanks to God. Our acts of kindness, integrity in work, and loving relationships all become expressions of worship when done for God's glory.

Obedience is a powerful form of worship. Jesus emphasized the importance of loving Him through obedience to His commands (John 14:15). Here, Jesus Himself said, "If you love me, you will obey my commandments."

Following God's Word, even when it is difficult, demonstrates our trust and submission to His will. Abraham's obedience to God was described as worship in Genesis 22:5. Abraham's willingness to sacrifice his son Isaac to God is considered a prime example of worship. Obedience reflects a heart fully devoted to Him and magnifies His glory in our daily lives.

Gratitude fuels a life of worship. By recognizing God's blessings and expressing our thanks, we cultivate a spirit of joy and reverence. 1 Thessalonians 5:18 encourages believers to give thanks in all circumstances, as this is God's will. Gratitude has the power to transform our ordinary moments into worshipful experiences, allowing our hearts to overflow with praise for His goodness.

Worship through music enhances our connection to God. Singing praises has been a part of worship since biblical times, as seen in the Psalms. Music stirs the soul, aligns emotions with the truth, and magnifies God's greatness. Ephesians 5:19 encourages believers to sing psalms, hymns, and spiritual songs, making music in our hearts to the Lord.

Worship involves surrender—letting go of our own desires and aligning our lives with God's purposes. In the Garden of Gethsemane, Jesus prayed, *"Not my will, but Yours be done"* (Luke 22:42), modeling the ultimate act of worshipful surrender. When we submit to God's authority, we invite His Spirit to work in us, transforming our hearts and lives.

Gratitude nurtures a life of worship.

By recognizing God's blessings and expressing our thanks, we cultivate a spirit of joy and reverence. 1 Thessalonians 5:18 encourages us believers to give thanks in all circumstances, as this is God's will. Gratitude has the power to transform ordinary moments into worshipful experiences, allowing our hearts to overflow with praise for His goodness.

I have discovered a principle that consistently helps me. Even in the most challenging situations, when worry tries to grip my mind, I make it a point to thank God for taking care of the current issue, like a family issue, and for His wisdom that comes to help me know what to do. Though worried thoughts may persist, I respond (guided by Philippians 4:6-7) by saying, "Thank you, Lord, for taking care of that, and I know what to do." I refuse to worry or be anxious. Thank you, Lord.

I have observed this principle work 99.9% of the time; the challenge dissolves, peace fills my heart regarding the issue, wisdom comes, and the challenge is resolved. God's word works!

Serving others is a reflection of a worshipful heart. As believers, our acts of love and service honors God by demonstrating His character to the world. Matthew 25:40 reminds us that whatever we do for the least of these, we do for Him. Therefore, our service becomes an act of worship, showing our gratitude for His love by extending it to others.

Corporate worship brings believers together to glorify God. Gathering with others to sing, pray, and study His Word strengthens our faith and nurtures the community. Hebrews 10:25 emphasizes the importance of meeting together to encourage one another. Collective worship enhances the joy and reverence of individual worship as our hearts unite in collective praise.

Living a life of worship transforms mundane moments into sacred opportunities. It aligns our every thought, word, and action with God's purpose. Worshiping in spirit and truth, as Jesus described in John 4:24, reflects a heart fully devoted to Him and following God's guidelines in His word on how He wants to be worshiped. For example, the psalmist (King David) said in Psalms 47:6-9 **Sing praises to God**, sing praises: Sing praises unto our King, sing praises. For God is the King of all the earth: **Sing ye praises with understanding**. Thus, according to God's Word, He is guiding us to Sing, to sing praises, and to do so with the understanding of His will and Word.

Once upon a time, in biblical times, King David danced and sang to God, but he did so without understanding. As a result, instead of bringing a blessing, death was released, and two people died. The story of Uzzah and the Ark of the Covenant can be found in 2 Samuel 6:1-7 and 1 Chronicles 13:9-12.

The ark was being transported on a cart pulled by oxen. When the oxen stumbled, a man named Uzzah reached out to steady the ark, but God's anger burned against him. He struck him down because Uzzah did not understand and violated God's Law, even though he was trying to help.

Wisely, King David sought understanding and, the second time, followed God's guidelines, which resulted in great prosperity—Understanding is crucial.

Another scripture, Psalm 100:4, says, "Enter His gates with thanksgiving and His courts with praise." This verse encourages us to come before God with a spirit of thanksgiving and to proceed to a deeper level; we praise Him. A life of worship glorifies God and draws others into His presence, making His greatness known throughout the world.

Reflection & Application – Living a Life of Worship

Worship is more than a moment; it is a lifestyle. True worship extends beyond church services into our daily lives, influencing our actions, thoughts, and relationships. Take time to reflect on how you can deepen your worship in all areas of life.

Reflection Questions

What does worship look like in your daily life?

Think about the ways you worship God outside of church. Are there areas where you can be more intentional?

- _____

- _____

- _____

- _____

- _____

- _____

LIVING A LIFE OF WORSHIP

How can you cultivate a heart of gratitude this week?

Consider how gratitude impacts your worship. What steps can you take to develop a habit of thanksgiving, even in difficult circumstances?

- _____

- _____

- _____

- _____

- _____

Are there any areas of your life where you struggle to surrender fully to God?

Surrender is a key part of worship. What might be holding you back from fully trusting Him?

- _____

- _____

- _____

- _____

- _____

In what ways can you use your talents and time as an act of worship?

Reflect on how serving others and using your gifts can be a form of worship.

- _____
- _____
- _____
- _____
- _____

How can you engage more deeply in corporate worship?

Think about how gathering with other believers strengthens your faith. Are there ways you can be more active in your church or faith community?

- _____
- _____
- _____
- _____
- _____

CHAPTER 12

Pressing On Toward the Goal

The Christian journey is a lifelong pursuit of knowing Christ and becoming more like Him. Pressing on through trials, temptations, and triumphs requires perseverance and focus on the ultimate goal: a deeper relationship with Jesus and eternal life with Him. The Apostle Paul captures this in Philippians 3:13-14, encouraging believers to forget what lies behind and strive toward what is ahead, pushing toward the goal of the heavenly prize in Christ Jesus.

The Christian life is not a sprint; it is a marathon. Spiritual growth requires endurance, which develops over time through reliance on God. Hebrews 12:1 encourages believers to run with perseverance the race set before us, shedding off every weight and sin that entangles us. By staying focused on this race, we ensure progress toward our goal, even when the path is difficult.

Trials and setbacks are inevitable, but they also present opportunities for growth. James 1:2-4 reminds us to consider it pure joy when we face trials, as they produce perseverance and maturity within us. God is not the author of confusion; however, when challenges arise, He uses them to refine our faith, deepen our trust, and strengthen our character. Pressing on requires faith in His purpose, even when the road is tough.

Focusing on Jesus provides us with the strength to face and overcome life's challenges. Hebrews 12:2 describes Him as the pioneer and perfecter of our faith, who endured the cross for the joy that was set before Him. By looking at His example, we can find inspiration for perseverance and confidence. Jesus overcame the ultimate trial, ensuring victory for all who choose to follow Him.

Letting go of the past is essential for pressing forward. Regrets, failures, and even past successes can hinder growth when clung to too tightly. Paul's exhortation to forget what lies behind does not mean ignoring lessons learned but releasing the weight of what no longer serves the journey ahead. Trusting God's redemptive power allows believers to move forward in freedom.

Community strengthens our perseverance. Encouragement, prayer, and accountability from fellow believers are essential during moments of doubt or fatigue. Ecclesiastes 4:9-10 emphasizes the strength of companionship, reminding us that two are better than one, and a friend can lift us up. Sharing the journey with others lightens our load and keeps our hearts focused on the goal.

Discipline is a crucial component of perseverance. Spiritual practices such as prayer, scripture reading, worship, and fasting help develop habits that sustain our faith. In 1 Corinthians 9:24-27, the Christian life is compared to a race, highlighting the importance of self-discipline in order to achieve the prize. Regularly practicing these disciplines not only offers physical and health benefits but also helps keep our hearts and minds aligned with God's purposes. Man is created to live not only on physical food but also on God's word.

Hope fuels our perseverance. The promise of eternal life and the presence of God's kingdom motivate us to keep moving forward. Romans 8:18 reminds us that the sufferings of the present time are not worth comparing to the glory that will be revealed in us. This eternal perspective encourages us to remain steadfast, even in the face of adversity.

Celebrating progress along our journey builds momentum.

Recognizing God's faithfulness, no matter how small our growth steps may be, strengthens our gratitude and determination. Milestones in our faith serve as reminders of His presence and power, inspiring us to continue pressing on with confidence.

I remember a time when I felt like my spiritual growth was at a standstill. I was praying, reading scripture, and trying to stay faithful, but it seemed like nothing was changing. Then, one day, I looked back at how I used to respond to challenges and realized how much God had strengthened me. The worry that once consumed me no longer had the same grip. Instead of reacting with fear or anxiety, I found myself **speaking God's Word instinctively, almost by reflex,** when a concerning thought or situation arose. It was at that moment that I saw how even small steps of faith were shaping me. That realization reminded me that God is always at work, even when we don't immediately see the results.

The ultimate goal is Christ Himself. Spiritual growth is about deepening our relationship with Him rather than seeking achievements or accolades. The prize of eternal life is not just a future hope; it is a present reality marked by His abiding presence. Pressing on toward this goal glorifies God and fulfills His purpose for every believer.

Persevering in faith allows us to turn our challenges into opportunities for growth, bringing glory to God in the process. Every step forward in this race, no matter how small, brings us closer to Him. By pressing on with hope, discipline, and reliance on His strength, we ensure that our journey leads to the ultimate prize of eternal life in Christ here on earth.

Conclusion
A Lifelong Journey of Growth

Christian growth is a lifelong journey of becoming more like Christ and deepening our relationship with Him. It is a path marked by trust, surrender, perseverance, and hope, guided by God's love and grace. Every step taken, whether through triumph or trial, brings believers closer to the heart of God and His eternal purposes.

The Christian journey requires intentionality. Growth doesn't happen by accident; it occurs through daily choices to seek God, abide in Him, and follow His will. Spiritual disciplines—such as prayer, scripture study, worship, and service—serve as tools to cultivate our vibrant and growing faith. These practices are not burdens but blessings that open the door to transformation and intimacy with God.

Challenges and setbacks are inevitable, but they serve a purpose. God uses difficulties to refine our faith, shape our character, and draw His children closer to Him. Even amid uncertainty, trusting in God's plans and promises builds endurance and reveals

His faithfulness. The trials we face become opportunities to experience His presence and power in new and profound ways.

The community of believers plays a vital role in this journey. Walking alongside others provides encouragement, accountability, and shared joy. Fellow believers strengthen each other's faith, offer perspective, and remind one another of God's goodness. The body of Christ, working together in love, reflects His heart to a world in need.

The goal of Christian growth is not perfection but transformation. It is about becoming more like Jesus—loving as He loves, serving as He serves, and living with the hope and joy He offers. It is about reflecting His light in a dark world and inviting others into the life-changing relationship He offers.

This journey is ultimately about a relationship—At its core, Christian growth is not about doing more or achieving more but about knowing God more deeply. His love is unchanging, His grace is sufficient, and His presence is constant. Every step of growth is our invitation to experience His love more fully and to trust Him more completely.

May this book serve as a guide and encouragement for your journey. As you trust God, abide in His presence, and press on through challenges, know He is with you every step. His plans for you are good, His purposes are eternal, and His love for you is unending.

This journey is not just about growth, but about becoming who God created you to be. May you walk forward with faith, hope, and confidence, knowing that "The Lord will bring to completion the good work He started in you" (Philippians 1.:6) Trust Him, grow in Him, and live for His glory.

Next Steps & Call to Action

Congratulations on completing this journey of faith! But remember—this is just the **beginning**. The Christian life is a lifelong pursuit of **growth, transformation, and deeper intimacy with God**. Every challenge, every victory, and every moment of doubt is an opportunity to **draw closer to Him**.

As you close this book, I encourage you to take action. Don't just **read** about faith—**live it**.

What's Next?

Here are some **practical next steps** to help you stay rooted in faith and continue growing:

Join a Bible Study or Faith Community – Surround yourself with believers who will encourage and strengthen you in your walk with Christ. Fellowship brings accountability, wisdom, and growth. *"As iron sharpens iron, so one person sharpens another"* *(Proverbs 27:17).*

Start a Faith Journal – Document your prayers, reflections, and lessons from Scripture. Writing down your journey helps you **see God's hand** in your life and strengthens your faith in times of doubt.

Share What You've Learned – Your testimony has power! Encourage someone else by **sharing** what God has done in your life. Give a friend this book, start a discussion, or simply share a verse that has impacted you.

Deepen Your Prayer Life – Commit to intentional time with God each day. Speak to Him, listen, and allow His voice to guide your steps. *"Draw near to God, and He will draw near to you"* (James 4:8).

Live Out Your Faith Daily – True transformation comes when we apply God's Word in our everyday lives. Walk in love, serve others, and **be a light** wherever you go.

Reflection & Application: A Lifelong Journey of Faith

As you reflect on what you've learned throughout this book, take a moment to reflect on what you've learned and how it can be applied to your life.

Key Takeaways:

What are the most important lessons God has taught you through this journey?

- _____
- _____
- _____
- _____

Next Steps:

What is one step you can take today to deepen your faith?

- _____
- _____
- _____
- _____

ROOTED IN FAITH

How can you actively live out your faith and be a light in your community this week?

- _____

- _____

- _____

- _____

Who in your life could benefit from hearing what you've learned?

- _____

- _____

- _____

- _____

Acknowledgments

First and foremost, I give all glory and honor to God, whose wisdom, grace, and faithfulness inspired and made this book possible. His guidance and presence have been my greatest source of strength throughout this journey.

To my family: your unwavering love, prayers, and encouragement have been a foundation in my life. Thank you for believing in me and supporting this calling.

I am deeply grateful to my friends and mentors, who have shared their wisdom and truth with me. Your insights, prayers, and uplifting words have shaped my faith and inspired this work.

To my readers, thank you for embarking on this journey with me. I pray that these words bring you closer to God and help you grow in your faith. May you find strength, hope, and encouragement on every page.

Finally, to everyone who played a role in the creation of this book—editors, designers, and publishing partners—your dedication and hard work have been invaluable. Thank you for helping to bring this vision to life.

May God bless you all abundantly.

About the Author

Paul Okwechime is a passionate Christian writer, speaker, and mentor dedicated to helping believers grow in their faith and deepen their relationship with God. With a heart for encouraging others through life's challenges, Paul shares biblical wisdom, personal experiences, and practical insights that inspire transformation and spiritual growth.

His faith journey has been shaped by personal trials and victories, along with a deep desire to walk closely with God. Through his writing, he aims to equip readers with the tools to navigate difficult seasons, trust in God's plan, establish God's kingdom on earth, and live out their faith confidently and purposefully.

When he's not writing, Paul enjoys creating, studying scripture, mentoring others, and engaging in meaningful conversations about faith and personal growth. His mission is to see lives transformed by the power of God's Word, helping others remain **rooted in faith** regardless of life's circumstances.

For more insights and encouragement, connect with Paul at (www.empoweredforwealth.com)

www.ingramcontent.com/pod-product-compliance
Lightning Source LLC
Chambersburg PA
CBHW070643030426
42337CB00020B/4148